oups

A Penguin Colony

By Autumn Leigh

Gareth Stevens
Publishing

Please visit our website, www.garethstevens.com. For a free color catalog of all our high-quality books, call toll free 1-800-542-2595 or fax 1-877-542-2596.

Library of Congress Cataloging-in-Publication Data

Leigh, Autumn, 1971-
 A penguin colony / Autumn Leigh.
      p. cm. — (Animal groups)
 Includes index.
ISBN 978-1-4339-8210-1 (pbk.)
ISBN 978-1-4339-8211-8 (6-pack)
ISBN 978-1-4339-8209-5 (library binding)
1. Penguins—Juvenile literature. 2. Social behavior in animals—Juvenile literature.
3. Animal societies—Juvenile literature. I. Title.
 QL696.S473L45 2013
 598.47—dc23

                                    2012021891

First Edition

Published in 2013 by
Gareth Stevens Publishing
111 East 14th Street, Suite 349
New York, NY 10003

Copyright © 2013 Gareth Stevens Publishing

Designer: Sarah Liddell
Editor: Greg Roza

Photo credits: Cover, p. 1 Josh Anon/Shutterstock.com; p. 5 Ronsmith/Shutterstock.com;
pp. 7 (emperor penguin), 15, 21 Jan Martin Will/Shutterstock.com; p. 7 (fairy penguin) Susan Flashman/
Shutterstock.com; p. 9 Richard Burn/Shutterstock.com; p. 11 Rich Lindie/Shutterstock.com; p. 13 orxy/
Shutterstock.com; p. 17 Grigory Kubatyan/Shutterstock.com; p. 19 Volodymyr Goinyk/Shutterstock.com;
p. 20 Gentoo Multimedia Ltd./Shutterstock.com.

Printed in the United States of America

CPSIA compliance information: Batch #CW13GS: For further information contact Gareth Stevens, New York, New York at 1-800-542-2595.

Contents

Boldface words appear in the glossary.

Social Birds

Penguins are birds that can't fly. They use their wings to swim instead—and they're very good swimmers! Penguins are some of the most social birds in the world. A group of penguins is called a colony.

5

Penguins of All Sizes

There are 17 penguin species, or kinds. Emperor penguins are the biggest kind. They can grow to be 45 inches (114 cm) tall. The smallest penguins are fairy penguins. They grow to about 17 inches (43 cm) tall.

emperor penguin

fairy penguin

7

Southern Living

Wild penguins are from the Southern **Hemisphere**. Many colonies are found where it's very cold. Penguins live on islands and along the coasts of South America, Africa, Australia, New Zealand, and Antarctica. They live near water so they can find food.

Where Penguins Live

Huge Colonies

Penguins often travel in small groups. However, they gather together in colonies to find **mates** and have babies. A single colony may have hundreds of thousands of penguins! One colony can cover an entire island.

Speak Up!

The many penguins in a colony all look the same, so they use sounds to **communicate**. This allows mates to find each other and their chicks in a crowd of penguins. They use sounds to warn each other of danger, too.

13

Move It!

Penguins also use special movements to communicate. These movements are called displays. After making a nest, males bob their head up and down. This is a call to females. It also warns other males in the colony to stay away.

15

Penguin Families

Female penguins lay one or two eggs once a year. In most species, the male keeps the egg warm while the female spends days or even weeks feeding at sea. When the female returns, it's the male's turn to feed.

17

Caring for Chicks

Adult penguins keep eggs warm by holding the eggs under their body and on their feet. When chicks break out of their eggs, they don't have heavy feathers like adults do. Both parents feed chicks and keep them warm.

Growing Up Penguin

When the chicks in a colony get a little bigger, they often group together. This keeps them warm and safe from enemies, such as hungry seabirds. After they grow up, many penguins return to the place they were born to have their own chicks.

Fun Facts About Penguins

The earliest penguin species lived more than 58 **million** years ago.

Penguin mates often stay together for life. Some stay together for just one **breeding** season.

A penguin colony is also called a rookery.

The largest penguin colony in the world is on Zavodovski Island in the South Atlantic Ocean. About 2 million chinstrap penguins call the island home!

Glossary

breeding: having to do with mating and giving birth

communicate: to share feelings or ideas through sounds or motions

hemisphere: one-half of Earth

mate: one of two animals that come together to produce babies

million: a thousand thousands, or 1,000,000

For More Information

Books

Molnar, Michael. *Emperor Penguins.* Mankato, MN: Smart Apple Media, 2012.

Schreiber, Anne. *Penguins!* Washington, DC: National Geographic, 2009.

Websites

Emperor Penguins

kids.nationalgeographic.com/kids/animals/creaturefeature/emperor-penguin/

Learn more about emperor penguins, see pictures, and watch a video of them.

PenguinWorld

www.penguinworld.com

Read much more about the penguins of the world.

Index